Kindli

the Light

within

Dedication

For the visionaries, entrepreneurs, writers, innovators and dreamers. Together, we can make the world a better place.

Contents

A diamond emerges

The world held me in
Its core.
The furnace of fire and
Pressure
Engulfed me.
Until my fingertips
Were but flames.
Consumed by a burning
Abyss,
I was forever stewing here.
Stuck in each moment of abuse.
I refused to make peace with the pain,
I so easily identified with.
Offering myself as fuel to the flames.
Time and time again.
Reborn a victim, even to myself.
By being afraid to move on.
Stuck in fear as though it was
Tar in a tar pit.
My extinction was here.
But something shifted,
I let the furnace burn out and
All imploded.
My core was transformed into
A dazzling diamond.
A strength beyond all comprehension.
I acknowledge that inner strength.
Shine on. Shine bright.

Share your love.
Share your story.
The darkest times in your life
Have shaped your wisdom,
Because you chose to learn the
Lesson presented to you.
Each challenge is an opportunity to grow.
To learn more about yourself,
How you view the world
And how you love others.
Forgive and let go.
You are not your pain.
It doesn't own you,
And you don't owe it
Any more time
Or attention.

The Coins in the wishing well

The coins in the wishing well,
Reflecting the sunlight and
the hopes of all
The wishes whispered, before the fall.

'Plop' a wish released,
To the unknown.
A prayer to be answered.
What did they wish for? I wonder.

Ah, but that is a secret to be kept.
Eager smiles floating all around,
Like smoke from blown out candles
On a birthday cake.
A happy, reminder of
Magical, childhood memories.

Coins in the wishing well.
Reminders that no matter what our age,
We are all playful children
At heart.
Wanting to have a little fun,
Before our time here, is done.

Book of life

No paper left.
I write small.
In the edges,
Like the groups fighting
For justice and peace.
Edges of life, swallowing lies.
To find some release
From hatred, pride and greed.
The desolation spreads.
They plant a seed of peace,
And each seed becomes a tree.
And those trees become a forest,
That grow until the edges of the sea.
Until all is leaf and relief.
From hopelessness and dread.
And the edges become whole pages,
And reach to the end.
And create a new book of life,
Completely free from hatred and strife.

Fierce Ones

Fierce ones,
That speak in tongues.
And hold your pen.
Razor edged.
In your soul, you do pledge.
I taketh and giveth
And send
Away.
The sad souls who never pray.
They have no Gods,
No true belief.
And from their own wretched
Souls, they find no relief.
They scream and howl
And wail in pain.
And yet do the same thing
Day after day.

No change of heart.
No change in being.
They seek outside,
Without ever truly seeing.
And in their blind ignorance, they drown.
Yet before their last breath,
They see the crown that
Was always atop of their own head.
In reach of their once living

Hands, now lifeless and dead.
This is a lesson to all,
Take a good look inside,
Before you commit to the fall.

Master of Puppets

Tanna, ecco, tabit, tut.
Relish that thy cannot cook,
The delicious recipe of life.
That you knew in the womb,
But got beaten out of you,
In the classroom.

A soulless automaton of the state,
An obedient soldier,
Served on the plate .
Of a staged war.
Oh, a waged war,
Contrived and prepared.
Illusions, controlled conclusions,
To which we thoughtlessly reacted.

The way they wanted us to react.
Controlled by the master of all puppets
And we never push back,
The curtain, to see ,
What play we are in.
The fool and the comic, and
The tragedy of whim.
Play on, then?
No harm, right?

Wrong. The master of puppets

Wants new puppets.
All of us,
We are gone.
Written off,
Outdated, tarnished, and
Without use anymore.
Tossed aside and thrown on
The floor.
Forgotten to history,
As they rewrote the books.
Look, new puppets to control,
With special hooks
Pierced into hearts and souls
To switch them off.
Just wooden shells of being.
All fight – given up!

Give me...

Give me the green, rolling hills
The undulating curves of
Mother Earth.

Give me the tantalising birdsong,
That is music to my ears,
Every time that I hear it.

Give me the delectable
Sweetness of wild raspberries and
Blackberries, freshly plucked, and
Eagerly tasted. Nature's divine recipe.

Give me the soft sunlight on my skin.
The trees that humble me.
The rivers which teach me to flow ever onwards.
The scent of pine needles in the forest.

Give me that evening light when all is quiet
And my thoughts cascade onto paper,
Like the branches of a weeping willow
Into water.

Speechless

Cast upon a desolate shore.
A land of fire and ash.
Green no more.
I soaked, in the salty sea.
Stood speechless
And grieving for there *were* ~~was~~ no tree*s*.

No trees for miles.
No trees at all.
When did all the mighty trees fall?
Did we do this?
With all our reckless hate.
Look now) Out of nothingness,
We can no longer create.

No shroud, no crown of thorns.

I ache, my soul it aches.
For all of humanity's mistakes.
The stinging, breaking toil.
That we must take and take
From the soil.
And no seed we plant.
Except that of hate.
What is this?
How can I escape?

Sad to be human.
No such gain. *Filled with shame.*
Forsaken of heart.
Mistaken of brain.

What caretakers are left?
The leaders enshrined. *Compassionate leaders*
We must seek them
And we must find.

Our saviours,
The Our light.
To guide the way.
Or to the unholy fires
Of death
We are but prey.
I speak truth, heaven sent.
If you do not change

And do not repent.

The reckoning will be here
Sooner than you think.
And into infinite darkness, we will sink.

I have no shroud, no crown of thorns.
I am but a gatekeeper of these words.

These words are forewarning of
Something that has already begun.

Put down your swords and stop
The sun.
In the ever-twisting deadly cycle.
For in your decay will you
Recycle,
Death with life.
And life with death.
Until there is nothing left.

The Boot

Fearful children, fearful ants.
What can you do?
Except be afraid of the boot,
Hovering above you.

A constant reminder of your
Pitiful excuse for an existence.

Aww, so sad.
I might but for a second,
Feel some sympathy.
Were it not for
The pathetic repetition
Of your mistakes.
And the acceptance of your oppressors.

I have one answer for you.
Cut it all down.
Your illusions, I mean.
And delusions,
Whatever you want to call them.

They have no place when you don't give them one.

Let the walls fall
And the boot
Was, but a butterfly in the wind.

Seed of Love

Seed of love,
Take root in my chest.
Grow and be cherished
In every breath.
And in every kind word.,
That I say so true.

From my heart,
For there love grows and grows.
It went beyond my fingertips
And past my toes.
Way beyond the reach of my nose.

And landed in the hands of the poor,
The ones who beg and knock on
The door of life,
And ask for love to
Answer back,
The seed was planted
And love prevailed.

It is an energy,
An enlivened state.
Something which we can all create.
When we see,
I am you and you are me.
We are all love in action and in being.

Shield Maidens

Shield maidens,
Heed my call.
We march together,
We march to war.

For our honour.
For glory.
We take back our power.
Heed the call.
This is the hour.

Shield maidens,
The horn is blowing
Upon the air.
Paint your face
And shave your hair.

Take up your sword and shield
Then And meet me in the blood
Soaked field.
We face the enemy
And forever fight.
Into the day
And beyond the night.

For Freya, for Thor,
I am Odin's kin.

And beyond this mortal realm,
We shall forever sing.

Shield Maidens,
Take up the call.
For we shall fight on
Forever.
And never shall we fall.

Home is where you are

Home is where you are,
The scent of you
Still wafting through the
Hallway as
You leave for work.

The papers all piled up,
Dishes in the sink.

Home is where you are,
My heart alive.
Eagerly pumping.
Your loving words
Around my body.

Sustaining me with an embrace.

Home is where you are,
Because to me
You are love encapsulated.

And the very essence of you,
Brings sheer comfort.

Outpace

I was eager to change, rearrange.

My hair, my face and furniture.

It just felt all over the place.

The expectations I held

Became hurdles

In a race.

Did I do that?

Try to outpace

The ticking of time.

With the eagerness of rhyme.

Age on the page.

Uneasiness in the creases and wrinkles.

The odd papercut.

As I find myself in tears,

Over the years.

Handle with Care

Your hate slit my wrists.
Your abuse tied the noose.
I am too soft and sensitive for
This rough and ready world.
Parts of me,
Have already caved in
From the 'not handled with care' moments.

Manifestation

Inhale, the dreams inside.
Exhale, limiting thoughts
As I connect to everything.
The cosmic, loving energy
Which embraces all.
I let that energy flow inside me.
I know that I am the smallest atom
And the largest star,
In a universe of stars.
I love.
I am loved.
I am a being of energy
And love.
My visions and dreams
Manifest before me.
I trust and I am grateful for the realisation
Of all my dreams and desires.

Middle Aged

I am beyond

Restless youth.

Yet far from old age.

The middle of the book.

Each day, the turning of a page.

Edging towards an ending.

Unknown and unclear.

The waters so changeable.

In every direction that I steer.

Solitary Comfort

Alone with myself is

Sometimes sweet.

Satisfying me like a marshmallow

Melting on my tongue.

Oh, the joyful stickiness

Of thoughts)

That float upon the

Air like my grandma's perfume.

Drifting as though dandelion seeds,

Floating too high to catch.

That is okay.

It is all okay.

The time is mine.

And it is all so easy, breezy.

Building Blasphemy

The empty, echoing church.

Where once grand services

Were held.

Filled to the brim with the faithful.

Now being surveyed,

For transformation into apartments.

Purchased by
~~For~~ the busy getting rich.

Better than becoming a night club,

I suppose.

Stone
How easy the angel falls,

Clattering upon the floor,

Like a prostitute's heels.

A job well done,

Everyone satisfied,

Except God.

Introvert

Introvert, long hours spent on projects, alone.
Oh, the joyous abandon
Into a world of words.
No feelings of being awkward. or
The pressure of saying the right thing.
Being so weary of people,   wary ?
As though they are sharp
Objects in a kitchen drawer.
Slice, dice and declare,
"No, I don't belong here".
Put me back amongst the books;
Solid and dependable books.
This pressure to be a people person irritates me.
A lake house, pen and paper.
That is me, happy forever.
All the hustle and bustle,
Meet and greet,
Small talk tussle.
Suits me not.

Gone Fishing

I sat with a fishing rod
By the lake,
Where I knew no fish lived.
I sat for hours, rooted
On the spot. ~~while~~
While Knowing that my efforts were fruitless.
And that the bait on the hook was useless.
I sat there nonetheless
And I hummed a happy tune,
Until the setting of the sun.
And the coming of the moon.
~~With the~~ midges biting at my face,
Yet still I sat.
Later, overcome with
Hunger and tiredness.
I fell to the floor.
My rod clattered
Into the lake and was no more.
And I slept under
The starry sky,
Deep and peacefully.
Then I awoke with sunlight's kiss.
I went to my shed and got another rod.
I made a sandwich,
And sat down on the edge of the lake .
And cast my rod into the water.
Large ripples,

Formed as it was cast, then
I relaxed into my usual position.

I was at peace – do you know how to do that?
Stop and do nothing.
It is a lot harder than it seems.
Try it and see.

Snake Eyes

The coldness like castle stone in winter,

The distance in your eyes, far away.

A child crying for "mummy",

As the bombs lead the world astray.

The loneliness brings a madness.—

Disconnected and torn from everything.

As though no one ever understands you,

They act confused by the words of the song that you
sing.

Way of Women

What part of the food chain are we on?

The one where our hands still toil

At home and at the office,

While tending to the children.

Bound in servitude.

Grateful for the scraps *that* we receive.

Scraps of love, time and power.

Maybe even control.

Until we wake up and realise,

It ~~really~~ does not need to be this way.

No longer pretty pawns

On the chessboard of life.

But fierce leaders,

Making bold moves,

That shake the current order.

A familiar face

Trapped in a place that you have no desire to be.

Surrounded by strangers' eyes.

Looks darting back and forth across the table.

Piercing and cold.

All you want is the warmth

Of a familiar face.

A friend willing to give you

A tender embrace.

To soften the hard edges of this

Life.

As you stab yourself to death

With dark thoughts and

Past horrors.

A familiar face would drown all that out.

And open the future out
out

Like a jasmine flower in water.

A smile transmitting the
Endless, trickling possibilities of love and life.

Gracefully growing old

I did not pin all my hopes

On staying forever beautiful

And
~~Or~~ young.

I knew youth would depart my bones,

There away, did you see it run?

I forget my age. It is this or that or

Something. A number.

Outside, the lines etch away.

Inside, I writhe.

My days are on the other side:

Counting down,

Not counting up.

Atrophy worsened by apathy.

And indifference.

The New World Order

Get rich or die trying.

Work and be grateful for

A holiday.

Watch Netflix during or after a commute.

Back and forth

Into cities filled with people, rubbish and rats.

Beneath the shining spires, statues of blind justice

And flags which fly.

It all cries —
~~Crying~~ out wealth will tie up

All that gloominess and poverty into a neat bow.

Quick fixes.

That is all this is;

Selling quick fixes,

Buying quick fixes.

We are addicts to our quick fixes.

What will yours be today?

New look

A blonde bob.

All neatly trimmed.

Looking great with my red lipstick.

Wearing a clean, cut suit with

Smart heels.

I am a businesswoman.

I burn my 'mum' jeans and fleeces.

And bobbles.

Then dive right in with the rest of the piranhas.

Only for me

Just have eyes for me, darling.

Have eyes, only for me.

Whisper your words of love,

Untainted and uncorrupted

By the scent of anyone else

On your skin.

On your lips.

Delight in me, honey.

Not some pretender.

They will never love you,

The way that I love you.

Just have eyes for me, darling.

Have eyes, only for me.

Call of the Wild

I am howling at the moon,

With my straggly hair

And dark circled eyes.

Bitten skin,

Burned from the sun.

A thirst in my throat

And a hunger in my belly so deep.

So deep.

Call of the wild.

Calling me back,

Calling me back.

The earth devours,

In the call of the wild.

Crimes of Passion

Love turned to lust,

Turned to hate.

A fierce, ferocious anger that tears

Into the core.

Loving and hating.

Hating and loving.

Ripping each other's souls out,

Until we don't know why we loved in the first place.

Maybe we are all children just

Playing pretend.

At life, love and everything else.

Committing our little crimes of passion

Italics

Until we die.

Cathedral

The coin rattles
In humble donation.
The candles lit,
Beneath your tortured image.
What prayers were asked of
In your name?

Each flame representing
A sacred message.
To entreat the most holy spirit.
In the name of...

Our vain, desirous and hedonistic ways.

Humbled by the vastness of these stone monuments,
Which appear immortal.

"Quiet now" the walls whisper.
The spirit is quiet.
Silence the chattering thoughts and
May peace be with you.

Artistic Motivations

Why did Picasso paint?
To release himself from the depths of poverty.
Nay. Piteous it would be,
For such a motivation.
His brushstrokes
Are guided by a higher hand.
He answered the spirits calling:
Expressing – love of the divine
And divine love.

I quietened my inner voice,
So, that I could hear the instruction.
Nay, not for glory, fame or delights. that _(it is)_
I shall write until the end of my days.
But For that kingdom,
That through my works,
The divine whispers-
"Mighty as you might appear in your finery, _realise_ _all_
that There is nothing more appealing than piety. ~~And~~
~~knowing that~~ all you do and achieve can only ever be
attributed to your maker.
Be humble evermore, for you are forever in his
presence".

Round and round

Round and round we go
Where we go, nobody knows.
Doorways past
And eyes windows,
Lazily spying inwards
And outwards.
Glutting forever,
In ignorant fury.

A splurge and scourge
Humanity.
Ambivalent in our love and hate-
For the earth, life and each other.

Toiling for what?
My feet ache as I search for answers,
My eyes weary from seeing more,
But not so much.
The busy city screams
At me with bustling bodies.
A pit of flesh,
Writhing and coiling
Around my spirit,
Like heavy chains.
Down I go.

now
Seeking home, the mundane

Kindling the Light within   Camille Smith

Routine until restless,
I go forth to seek more.

Round and round we go,
Where we go.
Nobody knows.

Unnatural Order

I feel the shift, the need to cast off
The unnatural order.
Life is messy.
Age is messier.
Love is a gaping, unfathomable pit,
That I keep falling into, unaware.

Self-acceptance or the realisation
That I am more than self.
The ego reigning like a
Reckless, insatiable beast.
Thus So, I write in hope that maybe
One day the beast will be tamed.

I don't feel like standing tall
Or speaking grand,
Pretending that I hold the world's
Knowledge in my head.
I get it wrong, make mistakes.

The divine are flawless,
Not I.   *are*
My imperfections on display.
Anxious and reclusive.
Socially inept.
Too many rules to navigate,
I will retire with my books.

Kindling the Light within   Camille Smith

No peacock feathers to display.

Confused by,
The need to be seen.
To know that I am alive.
Measured by another's gaze.
It seems foolish.

Or is it my ambivalence to being
Alone?
Delighting in the absence of
Chatter, yet desiring it.
Hours consumed by prattling on
About this or that.

Are we really seeking meaning
Or wishing our time away?
Not really knowing
Where we are going.
So, we are making it up as
We love, as we feed,
As we wage war
With our emotions, fists
And the chaos in our hearts.
That really, we are all hiding
From the true state of despair.

Solitary

Silently,
Less words fall.
Waxed, wearied and worried.
Faces all wrinkled,
The mirror
Is burdensome,
Hurried past now.
Dark circles formed
And life feels
Like, a traveller's heavy pack.
Too full of needless items.
Put something back.
Why is it not lighter?

I just want to hide
On an island _endlessly_
And write ~~and write and write~~
And die with a pen in my hand.
Contentedly

Rattling

The bus rattles
My thoughts rattle.
No rest.

The air conditioning rattles.
My thoughts rattle.
No rest.

Clatter, clank,
Whoosh, whack.
These thoughts spinning
Pushing me back.

Rattling in my head.

Wondrous Scenes

Wondrous scenes,

Stun me into submission.

Let me gaze

And chase them like a curious child.

Hold and release. ~~this~~ as though

Laughter upon a gentle breeze.

Endless And kisses on your forehead.

Of a love that is, forever yours.

Smile

Be here.

You belong.

Even if you feel

Different,

Disconnected,

You belong.

Hold hands with the earth

And dance amongst

Excited raindrops.

Smile because you are blessed.

And you sing the song of life.

An Unburdened Mind

Thoughts quiet.

Just a hush.

No rush.

Snow forming into slush.

I am formless like water.

Kissing the present moment,

As though every moment is forever.

Stretching outwards.

Ripe with opportunity.

Effortlessly being.

Thoughtlessly seeing.

An unburdened mind.

Resolve through suffering

See me. The scars that still tie me to the past.

Don't judge me by the pain I carry.

But by the dreams and love,

That I ~~have for today~~. *I hold today*

Despite it all.

My strength lies there.

Monument to love

Hold fast,

Hold on.

You are a monument to love.

A delightfully

Carved soul

Of darkness and light.

Casting shadows

That tomorrow

Will know of.

Silence kills

The Unnecessary.

Growth

Infinite hallways of the mind.

Finding my way across the divide.

Further from myself
And to myself I go.

To the beginning where the seed of love was once
sown.

Taking the acid from the soil, while
Ripping away weeds in my mind's toil.

Now I grow in grace.

Spreading loving roots,
Where hate now finds no space.

Peaceful Joy

Thoughts of the
Quiet, loving spirit
Planted.

The roots spreading deep
And firm,

Unshakeable.

I am unbound in the splendour
Of silence.

It is sunlight for my soul,

~~And with it all unfurls~~, beautifully.

Unfurling all

Acceptance

I accept myself.

I love you as I love myself.

A mirror image –

Thoughts and feelings reflected.

I seek to be

Love.

To radiate love,

Inwards and outwards.

Love for all, the darkness and the light.

For with acceptance comes peace.

Pour it out

I sat in my pain,
Like putting my finger
Into an open wound.
I let it tear
Open everything,
Until I felt like nothing.

Now I sit
And my sorrows
Are silent.
A relief
Settles upon me.

No chattering thoughts.
No urge to chatter.
No tearing at the walls.
No restless patter.

Just peace.
And I am
Gushing with gratefulness
Because feeling this way

Is AMAZING.

Passion project

What is your heart moved by?

Passion dancing within,
Taking the steps
In furious motion.

For love, hate or some other emotion.

What drives your passion?

Passion for yourself, others
Or beyond that.

Perhaps, a noble, higher calling.

Can you reach inside to find it? Can you sit still long
enough.

To hear, what has always been there.
Beyond the obstacles of inner fear.

Why are you alive?
What is your heart truly moved by?

Therein lies the answer, therein lies your path.

Visionary

A better humanity.
A world without weapons.
Compassionate people,
Building a legacy of love.

Caretakers, innovators and creators.
We level up together.
No borders.
No barriers.
A new way directed
From the heart.

This is the new currency
Trading in
Equality,
Quality while
Eradicating poverty.

Looking for ways to
Respect our environment.
Preserve, protect
And promote
Planetary
Love.

A collective – collectively
Loving and present conscious.

Minimalist
And aware
That every action
Has consequences.

Apathy is no longer an excuse.

Our eyes wide and fully open.
Turned towards
Uprooting the root of
Ignorance.

The visionary
Holds tomorrow,
By the persistence
Of plans made today.

Body, mind and soul – care

Do something for the body –

Exercise
Play
Run
Dance

Do something for the mind-

Read
Write
Create
Reflect

Do something for the soul-

Meditate
Be alone
Enjoy the silence
Go beyond self

Every day – to seek balance to feed the mind, body and soul.

Philosophy

My philosophy is unfolding.
Constantly shifting and
Evolving.

I enjoy the process of
Seeking, as much
As gaining an answer.

Each emotion has a place,
Guiding me higher.
Towards Back into my natural heart filled state.

Loving and still,
Content with now.
Yet obsessed with progressing
Each day.

Opening myself to the world.
Through ink,
The Lines of thought,
Drawn out.
This is how I pray.

Love Propagating

We can heal.
Become beings of love.
Then go and heal others
Propagating more
Beings of love.

This is the shockwave
Of change
That we have the power to create.

This is where we become:

One world. One humanity. One consciousness.

Progress is the by-product. Our evolution becomes
inevitable.

Noble hearts with noble goals,
Building a future that is, beyond bright.

Word Pit

I put the world to rights
In the stickiness
Of the words that I write.

You get caught up in them –
Railing and rallying.
Carving another path.
The distinctive justification.
In your life's simplification.
Caught up forever,
In words.

Mellow Yellow

Yellow, the all-encompassing mellow.
A chilled-out hue,
On a Sunday afternoon.
Easy going.

No tooing and frowing.
It is all yellow.
My wonderful, fine fellow.

Flowers, clothes, walls, ~~hair.~~ *and* *flare*
A life filled with yellow.,
Is one of ~~a lot~~ less care.

I am going to take this shade
And make some lemonade.
When life gives you yellow.
It is time to serenade.

Art service

One, two, three, four.
My life's now in my hands.
And I jump out of the door.

Into a theatre, full of music and dreams.
Here romance and tragedy
Rip at the seams.

In the script, the book, the poem, and the song.
Words of the thinkers, be they right or wrong.
Now spoken aloud.
Dumbfounding, shocking and
Silencing the crowd.

The beloved ears – the silent masters
Of our craft.
Their approval, becoming our a life raft.

Well, we all serve each other in some way.
Brothers, sisters, lover to lover parents, lovers
And to the God(s) that we pray.

Emotion Sickness

Frustration, hurt, pain
And fear.
Spewing forth like emotional diarrhoea.

My mind closed as though
A clenched fist.
Ready to hit.

But I only beat myself up
With this anger,
Slowly sinking in a tar pit.

Circling, cycling
From calm to seething.
Back to being barely here.
Barely breathing.

What is this?
Why do I keep coming back to feeling this way?
I just want to heal
And stop feeling such dismay.

Self-love

I am giving it all to myself,
The good stuff.
Self-love brimming over,
Like a glass of ~~coca~~ cola.

I am giving myself inner smiles.
The ones so full and wide.
And I am holding on
To all the happiness inside.

I decided, ~~what is the~~ there's no point in feeling glum.
We are all headed in the same direction.
It is better to die happy.
Enjoy the journey, not just the destination.

Life Health and Safety

Please mind your head.
Mind the thoughts in your head.
So that they don't internally bruise you
Into apathy or depression.

Please mind the gap.
Mind the gaps in your knowledge.
Knowing that you are just as
Ignorant as the person next to you.
Stay humble.

Please take care on the stairs.
As you travel up or down in life.
Hold onto the handrail because
Regardless of which way you are
Going, you will need some stability.

Map: You Are Here.
Trust your inner GPS.
It will guide you where you need to go.
Believe that right in this moment.
This is where you need to be.

Stay away from the platform edge.
The edges of existence.   over them
You might push yourself too close
And plummet to your death.

73

Witnessed only by the pigeons.

CCTV covers all areas.
Be aware. In a state of constant awareness.
In this moment, otherwise you might miss out.

Please mind the closing doors.
You might not get another chance.
To go through them again.
Missed opportunities can sting
For a lifetime.

Caution: Wet Floor.
You may slip up on your own emotions,
If you don't make the effort to regulate them.
Sometimes a good cry is the healthiest thing to do.

Stop! Curb the negativity

What do you achieve from beating yourself up?
A headache, a grim expression and
An always empty cup.

Stop! Curb those negative thoughts.
They only bring you despair.
As you think them, you feed them
while About you they have no care.

Fill yourself with joy:
Go love, create and eagerly live.
Make mistakes and have passion.
But remember to forgive,
~~Yourself and other~~s.

For we all project our pain.
I am you,
You are me.
We are all one and the same.

Let's curb the negativity
And replace it with
Positivity.
It isn't much harder to think this way.
Have hope and faith,
You deserve a better today.
You can give yourself that with

A simple shift in thinking.
That way through life you'll be floating
Instead of sinking.

It is all worth it

Your ideas, dreams and visions.
The world you seek to create.
It is all worth it.
And it never is too late.

Go commit yourself to something that you love.
Invent, create and explore.
It is better to dream big,
Than to watch your dreams float
Out of the door.

Carve a new path, one that you choose.
Because life is hard no matter what path we tread.
So, it is better to live a life you love. and
Leave a legacy to live on after you are dead.

It is all worth it.

Nature's Way

I notice that nature meanders.

    It floats and flows.

It basks and sings.

There isn't the heavy, aggressive

     Grasping

That leaves one anxious to

Keep up in the race.

     There is no race.

There is only life and living it.

What If?

If I don't do it,

I will always be wondering

"What if?"

And it is the "what ifs?" that seem to

Haunt me forever.

I don't want that anymore.

Even if it means taking a complete leap of faith.

I would rather leap than drown under

The awesome weight of "what if?" "What if?"

"What if?"

Caramel Kisses

Caramel kisses, sweetness defined.

Hopeful reminisces, always on my mind.

Our dreams are all wispy and light.

Remember baby, hold on tight.

The world's hard edges

Now all gone.

I can only capture your sweet,

Softness in song.

Salty Defeat

What do you do when you are barely here?
Buried in torment, drowning in fear.
And your heart is beating like
A Hummingbird's wings.
It takes all your courage to
Fight against so many things.
You want to be strong,
But you worry your strength is running low.
With all the battles you fought,
What victory can you show?
The dried tears on your face
Crusted and cracked –
A salty defeat.
You must fight on, fight on.
Find a new level,
Find your feet.
Land somewhere good,
Take yourself there.
Strip yourself of everything
And lay yourself bare.
Stare into the darkness and scream at your howling
fears.
Then realise it wasn't worth any of your tears.

Waste Culture

So many people,
With so many things.
A consuming and wasteful society.
Truly careless as to what this brings.
It will bring drought, famine, suffering and pain.
The greed blinds us all,
Believing our life will always be this way.
That the wildfires are just a fluke.
That the biggest threat is an unused nuke.
We really don't need to consume so much.
We are not in tune with nature, we are completely out
of touch.
Let's go back to basics,
So, we can all survive.
Maybe this way
The earth will thrive.
Sustainable communities
Working as one.,
Attempting to fix the damage that's been done.

Passion for life

You can lose everything.

And you'll still be alive.

With your guts and your glory.

And your passion to be ALIVE.

That is all you need.

Surely dear, that is all you should feed.

Slippery Feelings

I pour my heart out,

Spew it like seaweed on slippery rocks.

I then become as gentle as the lapping

Waves upon the shore.

The Sand Fairies

As the sun sets on the vast, empty beach.

And the sea invades the shore.

There is a light, faint glow.

That you may glimpse

If you are very still and watch carefully.

Behold, the Sand Fairies, as they delicately dance over
dark wisps of seaweed.

They eagerly seek

Architectural delights.

The ones many hands have sculpted,

With joy, laughter and excitement.

Hands of different sizes,

Holding spade and bucket.

The proud builders,

Creators by the sea.

That is what Sand Fairies seek.

Sandcastles:

Grand ones,

Ruined ones,

Single, multiple and

With moats.

Some with flags

Or decorated with pebbles and shells.

They gather, admire and celebrate.

The wondrous creations of sand.

So, if you spot the flickering glow

Or see tiny footprints

In the sand.

Just know that the Sand Fairies are about.

Mother Earth

She holds the Earth in a
Watery embrace.
Her dark eyes shining upon
An ancient, cracked face.
Worn and withered
In her wisdom and pride.
She spins and spins
And never leaves our side.
Mother Earth,
Holding us afloat,
Will her tears drown us?
Because of our severe lack of care
As we glut on her resources
And do so little to prepare.
Her hands cannot
Spin this world when it is on fire.
And her tears cannot put out the flames
Of our carelessness,
As we build our own funeral pyre.

Old Soul Partner

Two old soul partners meet,
as they have met before –
summoned towards each other,
door after door after door.

Imagine tomorrow your old soul partner
arrives and for reasons beyond understanding
you are drawn together, like strong magnets, those
fierce vortices spinning attraction in every atom of your
being.

When you look into their eyes,
it is as though, every previous memory
you had together plays out, permeating decades,
centuries, millennia.
There you unite on the battlefield, the
hundreds of battlefields of life.
Where you have waged wars:
with your love,
with your hate,
with your anger, betrayal and grief.
The whole stinking lot of life with hot
blood in your veins.

The tears, the laughter, the pain.
They are but collateral damage

from the very raw, brutal and
eternal chains which pull two
old soul partners together.

Two destinies weaved, reconnecting
as though the powerful lay lines of love
finally align and flow.

That is why when you see your old soul
partner, your heart skips a beat as mine does
when I look at you.

I see it deep in your eyes,
I hear it in your voice.
The very presence of you
is an exciting familiarity,
wrapped in the glorious inevitably
of love across many centuries.

So, as you come through the door,
I sigh old soul partner, "my fate is sealed
once more".

The Hour of the Wolf

I hear your howl upon the edge
of daylight's last embrace.
Your fur glistening by moonlight's kiss,
as you hunt, long into the frozen night.

Between the trees I see the glint
of your ferocious stare,
so still, so untameable,
filled with bloodlust.

In your predatory stare – my flesh is
dismembered, instantly.
But you see, I am part of your pack
and that death glint is replaced
by a fierce, primordial loyalty.

Your powerful presence nurtures the fearful
psyche to be released, reborn
from the dark growl into the stoic state.

Now I embrace the hour of the wolf
and summon that luminous spirit:
to let light shine from my old wounds and
let it tear up my scars until I am released,
like a howl into the quiet night.

The Gallery

I stood, in awe while squeaks echoed across the shiny, buffered floor.

And quiet mutterings bless the hooked portion of the artist's mind, which by their enigmatic strokes you are hung, wanting more.

The Collective

Newspaper prophets swaying empty minds to
ignorance.
Fear sells, hate sells.

Humanity digresses.

Yet deep within the core of every person lies a seed of
goodness, which when nourished by hope and love,
grows vastly.

Humanity progresses.

As a collective unburdened by greed, power and
corruption and instead inspired by the common good.

We can achieve anything.
We can achieve everything.

Through saving each other, we save ourselves and the
world we share.

Star Quality

All the furs in the world couldn't save you or your
diamonds or jewelled rings.
Because if you're broken inside, you have nowhere to
hide and you know the world won't owe you a thing.

Take back your power darling, take back all your
dreams. Don't sell them to the highest bidder, be proud
and be seen.

You can transform the darkness from all the hurt, pain
and fear into a bright, radiant, star quality, my dear.

Message Received

Last text message: I love you all.

The last moments of life, desperately
hanging on.
The rubble encloses me now, like a dusty tomb.
The echo of gunfire, muffled, drowned out by a mighty
BOOM!

This is someone else's fight; for greed, for power, not
for me.
I am one of the **365 now dead** scrolling across breaking
news on your TV.

Can you hear that? My daughter is crying "mama" to a
ghost.
Who will wipe her tears?

To the leaders – is this your victory?
Blood spilled, numbers in, as you celebrate over beers.

Metamorphosis

Crawling, sprawling, creeping and eating – the
caterpillar gorges itself. Preparation for metamorphosis.

It builds a cocoon, the haven of solitude and
disintegrates itself into cellular mush – completely
broken down.

Time passes and the cocoon breaks apart, a butterfly
emerges with beautifully coloured wings, shining
brightly in the sunlight.

It flutters lightly upon the breeze, dancing from flower
to flower and sipping on the sweet nectar of life.

A painful rebirth.

Growing, living, loving, feeling and consuming. The
human gluts on experiences in preparation for
transformation.

It retreats inside a darkened room in solitude. There it
cries out in pain, the faulty thought patterns
disintegrating – completely broken down.

Kindling the Light within   Camille Smith

The human after some time opens the curtains,
windows and doors – letting the light in. It emerges,
breaking free from past pain and trauma.

It now walks in love and joy with a bright, dazzling smile.

A painful rebirth.

Words Unsaid

My friend said, "I feel so low that I want to die".

It struck such sadness into my heart.
I didn't know what to say or where to start.
I wish that I had said:

"I understand. I have felt this way too. It is okay.

Your pain won't dissipate if you keep fighting it or
numbing it away.

Accept that it is part of you – feel it, you don't have to
fear it, fight it or run from it anymore.

Overcome it, don't let it drag you to the floor.

You are so beautiful and magnificent; it would be a
dreadful loss if you left.

You can't see yourself as others do, without your good
and tender heart, we'd be bereft.

Your sharp mind and intelligence are an inspiration,
you're a leader, boundless and powerful, a most
majestic creation.

Kindling the Light within   Camille Smith

We all love you.
We are all here for you.
You don't have to carry this pain alone.

With us, you have a forever family.
You'll always have a home.

So please don't forget that,
Whenever you feel low.

You belong here, are loved here and wherever you may
roam".

Sacred Dimensions

Maybe you'll be my great love.
But I'll let time show me and that is enough.

I cannot bend all these wills and the universe with them.
Just got to let it be, enjoy my time and savour the
moment.

Take a dive into your bright, blue eyes.
And try not to surface.

You'll teach me the song of love – note by note.
Rising in tempo, until we kiss in sacred dimensions.

The Spirit of the Earth

The spirit of the earth
Is deep in despair,
Choking on pollution while
Gasping for clean air.

The spirit of the earth
Is screaming in pain.
As wildfires burn forests away.

The spirit of the earth
Is buckling under
The weight of waste,
While thirsting for water.

The spirit of the earth
Will burn away,
As our climate heats up
Day after day.

The spirit of the earth
Is drowning, as storms rage
And ice caps are melting.

The spirit of the earth
Is taking a final breath.
We failed to be good caretakers
And now we all face death.

The Fabric of Life

Weaver, you wanted to weave
All the colours of nature
And wear them on your skin.
As though you carry the
Sky, the sea and wild wondrous
Landscapes with you.
This is your reminder,
That the earth is always with you.
A forever friend,
That spins with you.
As you spin your loom.

Energise

Flow, flow
Aligned with a
Happy resonance.
Tapping into
Higher frequencies
That energise.
You flow excitedly,
Full of life,
Unbounded and fearless.
Taking it all as it comes.

All is light, colour and sound.
I am part of that.
I carry and emit my own light
As part of divine creation.

All things in balance

The sweet valleys are calling
Me home.
And your love will be with me,
Wherever I may roam.

Over lochs and rivers,
I will soar like than eagle wise.
And forever in my memory,
I will hold your sparkling eyes.

Across this land so lush and green.
It makes my heart burst in song.
Don't fret love, I'll be with ye.
The wait won't be long.

And I will kiss you as softly as the light
Embraces the earth.
All things in balance,
In passing and in birth.

Scotland

Vast land of thistle and heather.
Flowing to many lochs, full and deep
And wide.

Here lies Scotland's glory.
This fine country,
Holds high its pride.

And my heart that ever dwells here.
Swells with love amongst the fair hills
And vales.

A waking dream, as I am wandering
Around the castles, full of tales.

And the flowers are blooming,
Framing palaces and ruins.
Preserving a special history,
From Latin inscriptions to Celtic runes.

The standing stones aligned under the
Bright, milky way.
And the sacred Rosslyn chapel,
Where I hang my head and pray.
A land of mystery beauty and song.
Scotland, I love you.
It is here that I belong.

Shock waves

Let's be shock waves.
Not ripples.

Let's be radical change.

Shouted out.
Not whispered.

Printed in Great Britain
by Amazon

85520631R00061